JOHN ASHMAN FRPS
RAIL PORTFOLIO

A pleasing action shot of 'Castle' No. 7037 *Swindon* accelerating away from a Reading stop, past the East Junction with an 'up' train – the line to the Southern just visible in the foreground. I particularly liked this signal gantry which was situated close to East Main box. This picture like many others in the book, was taken with the Mentor Reflex camera fitted with a $6\frac{1}{2}$ in Tessar lens, and the enlargement has been made using only a portion of the 6 in x 4 in glass plate for maximum impact.

JOHN ASHMAN FRPS
RAIL PORTFOLIO
COMPILED BY MIKE ESAU

Haynes

Oxford Publishing Co.

John Ashman Hon. FRPS.

A FOULIS-OPC Railway Book

© 1988 Jonathan Ashman, Mike Esau & Haynes Publishing Group

Published by:
Haynes Publishing Group
Sparkford, Near Yeovil, Somerset. BA22 7JJ

Haynes Publications Inc.
861 Lawrence Drive, Newbury Park, California 91320, USA

British Library Cataloguing in Publication Data

Ashman, John
  Rail portfolio.
  1. Locomotives
  I. Title   II. Esau, Mike
  625.2'6
  ISBN 0-86093-416-0

Introduction

This is a picture of Maurice Earley and myself at Reading on a railway photographic session just after the last war, in about 1946 I think. We are both using large plate cameras which needed the support of a firm tripod, and although the results were very good, the equipment was not versatile enough for us to be very adventurous in our approach to the subject – auto focus and metering, motor drive and so on were unknown, high quality 35 mm and medium format cameras were only in limited supply and very expensive at that.

But how did my interest in railways and railway photography start? Although there were no railwaymen in our family, I must have liked railways from my earliest years, and perhaps this was fired by the large wooden engine my parents bought me when I was small and which I spent many happy hours pushing around the house. In those days we lived near the station at Earley on the outskirts of Reading. Earley was on the joint LSWR and SECR line which divided at Wokingham to run in one direction to Guildford and the other to Ascot thence to Waterloo. It was on this line during the First World War that I saw my first real trains at Mays Bridge which crossed the line by a bridge near Earley station. It is amazing how clearly names of locomotives stick in the mind so many years after, for I recall troop trains for Aldershot hauled by GWR 'Badminton' 4-4-0s, with dignified names like *Grosvenor, Alexander Hubbard* and *Monarch*. To my young eyes these Great Western engines were far more interesting than the anonymous LSWR and SECR types which hauled most of the trains on this line. In later years I always had a soft spot for the various sorts of GWR 4-4-0s, especially the 'Duke' class, and one of my most treasured pictures of two of them double-heading a train on the Cambrian Section, appears on page 8.

As I grew older and my horizons widened, I ventured further afield to discover the Great Western main line at Colebrooks Farm Bridge where I spent many happy hours locospotting, though of course there was far less information on trains, locomotives and their workings than there is today. One of the best locations to see trains was Reading General station, and it was here that I met other enthusiasts, including the youthful Maurice Earley and Cecil Blay. They were a little older than I

and both had cameras. Their enthusiasm and encouragement to me was such that I persuaded my father to buy me a 5/- (25p) Box Brownie taking $3^1/_2$ in x $2^1/_2$ in film which then cost 1/3d (about 6p) a roll, quite a lot of money for me in those days.

The station staff at Reading were very tolerant of us provided we were quiet well behaved chaps who did not get in the way of passengers, and left us to enjoy the constant procession of trains. The biggest engines in 1922 which I could find in my copy of *Great Western Engines, Names, Numbers, Types and Classes* were the 'Saint' and 'Star' class 4-6-0s, plus the various types of 4-4-0s. I was therefore very excited when I saw for the first time No. 111 *The Great Bear*, the GWR's only Pacific.

I took this picture of the engine at Reading in 1922 using the Brownie, and it is from the original 6 in x $4^1/_2$ in print which I made using a daylight enlarger. This enlarger was a fairly crude affair, the negative being inserted at the top and Kodak 'Velox' paper in the bottom. The loaded paper was given quite a long exposure in even daylight, then developed and fixed in the usual way. Later on I bought a proper enlarger, the illumination for which was provided by an incandescent gas mantle inside the top housing. The mantle was lit all the time the enlarger was in use, and the light controlled by a shutter to let it through to the paper below as required. When we had electricity at the house I converted the enlarger to take a conventional lamp which made work a lot easier. Of course, photographic paper was a lot slower in those days and did not lie flat once developed like modern resin coated material. At least the slow paper meant that a room need not be absolutely light tight for developing prints.

Looking back I think that had I not been fortunate enough to meet other railway photographers at Reading, notably Maurice Earley, my accomplishment and interest in the subject might never have developed. As is well known, Maurice started the Railway Photographic Society in the early 1920s, and I became one of its earliest members, in about 1923. There was a wealth of well known names in the Society over the years, and through it I met Ernest Wethersett, Cyril Herbert,

H. Gordon Tidey, Frank Carrier, Lewis Coles, and Frank Hebron (whose work I always admired), among others. The work of many of them is now recorded in OPC's splendid book *Steam Cameramen* which member Brian Morrison put together so well. The pictures which circulated in the RPS postal portfolios were of tremendous interest to me and a spur to improve my own work.

By the mid 1920s I had become very keen on railway photography, and bought my first good camera, an Ensign Cameo which took 3½ in x 2½ in glass plates. Some of the pictures in the book were taken with this camera. The picture below, which again is from my original print, shows 'King Arthur' No. 773 *Sir Lavaine* on a 'down' boat train near Hook, and was the first picture I had published, appearing in *The Wonder Book of Railways* in 1927.

The RPS would sometimes have outings to attractive locations for a photographic session, and here is a snap which I have retrieved from my album, of myself, Maurice Earley (in the large trilby) and Signalman White, during a visit we made to Greenwood box on the LNER main line in the late 1920s. I am carrying my Salex reflex camera in its leather case. Everyone seemed to wear a hat in those days and I particularly remember F.E. 'Fred' Mackay, one of the 'grand originals', who was always smartly turned out with a bowler.

After the war I bought a Mentor reflex camera using 6 in x 4 in glass plates and fitted with a Tessar lens and focal plane shutter moving from the top to the bottom of the film plane. The shutter speed was regulated by the width of the slit, and for moving trains I found that a one eighth of an inch at f8 in sunshine using HP3 film developed in May & Baker Promicrol was just right for most moving trains. The shutter speed would have been about 1/500th to 1/750th of a second. With the slit wide open a slow speed equivalent to about 1/10th of a second could be achieved. Combined with the weight of the glass plates, this was a very heavy camera, and modern 35 mm photographers will no doubt be astonished to know that in general I would only take about six pictures on an outing. With so many steam trains about one could afford to wait for a good smoke effect, or perhaps a rare engine.

The big negatives enabled me to make large exhibition size prints, and encouraged by the Reading Camera Club, I successfully submitted a panel of twelve landscape and railway subjects for my Associateship of the Royal Photographic Society, followed by a Fellowship in 1952, and am still an honorary member of the Society. The preparation of these big prints gave me a lot of satisfaction, and during a darkroom session I might make only two or three which I was satisfied with. They were mounted by means of a heavy old mounting press heated by gas jets, which I could hardly lift. The mounting board, mounting tissue, print and protecting sheet were placed in the heated press, which was screwed down to provide sufficient pressure to bond the print to the board. The result was invariably first class and the prints are as good today as when I made them.

After the war I started a long and happy association with the Publicity Department of the GWR, and later British Rail Western Region. I was lucky enough to be given a lineside pass for certain stretches of line which included Whiteball and Dainton Banks, and I was very pleased when several of my pictures were used in their famous *Holiday Haunts* publication, as well as for many other publicity purposes as time has passed. When steam finished for good on the Western Region and I no longer had a darkroom through moving into a flat, I gave up black and white work to concentrate on colour, which in any case the Western Region by then preferred for publicity purposes. But I have remained faithful to larger format cameras and now use a Mamiya twin-lens reflex using either the standard or telephoto lenses and loaded with Ektachrome film.

Although most of the features I knew in steam days have gone, such as semaphore signals, the challenge to produce good pictures is, if anything, much greater. Trains are more uniform, there are fewer of them, and they run at such high speeds that even the stopping power of modern camera shutters are tested, especially when using comparatively slow colour transparency film.

Nevertheless the basic ingredients for a good picture are still there, even if not so rich and varied as before, and it still gives me a great deal of satisfaction to be in a pictorial location with interesting lighting on the subject.

Many of the pictures could not have been taken without the facilities provided by the Western Region which has enabled me to pursue my hobby and help them at the same time – I am most grateful to all my friends there, past and present. I also have to thank Mike Esau, without whom this book would not have been possible, and in particular for printing all the pictures so splendidly, and for writing the picture captions for me, based on taped conversations we have had together.

Even after all these years I had never seen some of my negatives in print form, and the wonderful memories that come back to me whilst looking at the pictures in this book, are as clear as if it were yesterday.

John Ashman
Reading
January 1987

I was on holiday for a week in Somerset in 1955 with a friend, Ernest Rixon, and wanted to get some pictures of this fine gantry of Great Western signals at Norton Fitzwarren. I was particularly pleased to capture this passing fitted freight, hauled by 9F class 2-10-0 No. 92205 from Bristol (St. Philips Marsh) shed. This engine was one of the first batch of engines built at Crewe in 1954, and in this picture appears to be in almost new condition.

Two 'Duke' class 4-4-0s near the top of Talerddig Bank in 1929 with a nine coach train for the North. The leading engine is No. 3276 *St. Agnes* and the train engine No. 3264 *Trevithick*. I was very fond of the 'Dukes', and I believe some 20 odd were drafted over to the Cambrian section of the GWR to replace the original Cambrian 4-4-0s. Apart from the motive

power I think this scene is almost unchanged to this day, though there is now much more lineside vegetation. This picture was taken with an Ensign Cameo camera fitted with a Ross Xpres lens, producing a $3^{1}/_{2}$ in x $2^{1}/_{2}$ in glass plate.

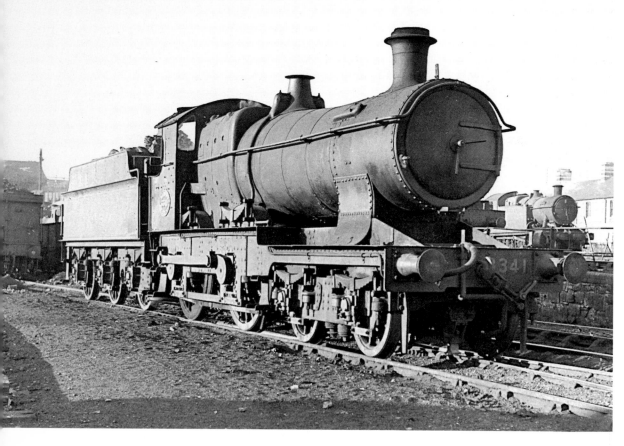

'Bulldog', No. 3341 *Blasius* at Newton Abbot shed in the 1920s during a holiday I spent in the West Country. Whenever possible I always liked to use the light to the best advantage to enhance the lines of a locomotive as in this picture. In the other picture, a 'Bulldog' No. 3313 *Jupiter* from Newton Abbot shed, is seen at work on a typical duty, piloting a 'King' on the 'down' "Cornish Riviera Express" made up of Centenary stock, nearing Dainton Summit in 1937.

Another "Bulldog', No. 3396 *Natal Colony* at Reading on station pilot duties in 1947. The engine looks rather run down after service during the war and was withdrawn the following year. This was a rare engine at Reading and was shedded at Bristol at the time I believe. The nameboard behind the engine is typical of the pattern that could be seen at any large GWR junction station.

'City' class No. 3705 *Mauritius* is pictured in 1926 at Reading on station pilot duties, and compared with the picture of No. 3396 the scene had not changed much over the years.

0-6-0ST No. 1337 *Hook Norton* at Weymouth in 1925. I took this picture with a Kodak Autographic Brownie camera whilst on a holiday with my parents, and remember sneaking into the shed to get it, although the first engine which caught my eye was 'Bulldog' No. 3373 *Sir Willian Henry*. *Hook Norton* was built in 1889 by Manning Wardle and had a varied career. The locomotive worked for the Hook Norton Ironstone Partnership Ltd until sold to the GWR in 1904. In 1907 it went to the Fishguard & Rosslare Railways & Harbours Company to undertake duties at Fishguard Harbour, but came back to the GWR in 1913. After this it spent the majority of its time working at Weymouth harbour until withdrawn in 1926.

As I have mentioned in the Introduction, I started work like many railway photographers with a Box Brownie camera, which was used for this picture of the only Great Western Railway Pacific, No. 111 *The Great Bear* at Reading station in 1922. The engine is standing on the 'up' relief line in No. 6 platform with a train from Weston-Super-Mare and Bristol, while the signal indicates that it is to join the main line.

'Star' class No. 4001 *Dog Star* in lovely condition at Reading shed in the late 1920s. To my eyes the 'Stars' were the best proportioned of the GWR 4-6-0s. This picture was taken during a visit to the shed with Maurice Earley. I don't remember much about the other picture, but it shows 'Aberdare' No. 2612, if I remember correctly, at Wolverhampton in 1928 during a shed visit with my friend Douglas Rumble.

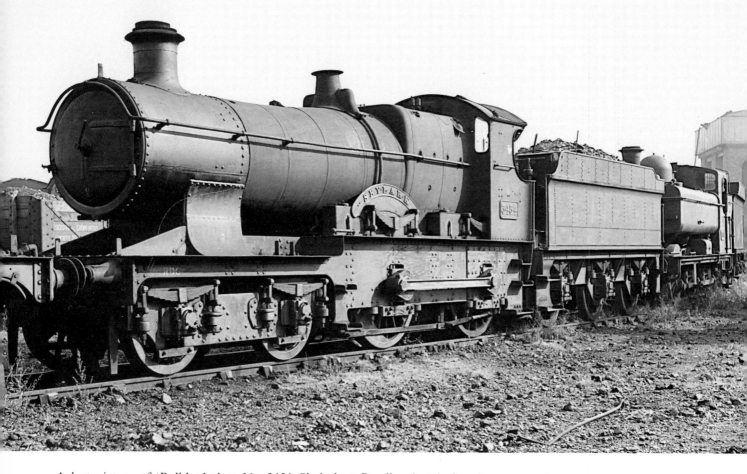

A last picture of 'Bulldog' class No. 3454 *Skylark* at Reading just before it was sent for scrap to Swindon. This engine and sister locomotive No. 3453 *Seagull* were both shedded at Reading at the end of their days, and were scrapped at the same time in November 1951. The other picture, which is so typical of the GWR, shows two 'Saints' at Reading shed in the 1920s. At the front is No. 2920 *Saint David* and behind No. 2937 *Clevedon Court*, both of which were among the last of the class in service.

The SECR Reading to Redhill line ran almost along the end of my garden at Earley. Here is the Birkenhead-Dover-Deal through train, which we called "The Continental", composed of GWR clerestory stock passing Earley at about a quarter past one, hauled by Stirling F1 class 4-4-0 No. A9. Of the many trains which used this line every day, this was one of the most interesting, and I tried to make a point of seeing it when I could. The smoke was not arranged, just good luck!

L12 4-4-0 No. 425 on the climb from Brockenhurst Junction to Sway with a train from Brighton to Bournemouth. Although the engine was built in 1904, and at the time the photograph was taken in 1937, far from modern, its clean and well cared for appearance with burnished buffers, is noteworthy. I remember that the next train to come along was hauled by 'Lord Nelson' No. 857 *Lord Howe*.

This Adams X2 4-4-0 No. E 590 from Eastleigh shed looks exceptionally elegant with its 7 ft 1 in driving wheels. Pictured on Reading shed in the late 1920s after working into the town with a train from the Basingstoke line. The engine survived until 1937 and was one of the last of the class to be withdrawn. This visit to the shed was made using one of the shed permits which in those days the Great Western Railway issued for 2/6d (12^{1}/2p).

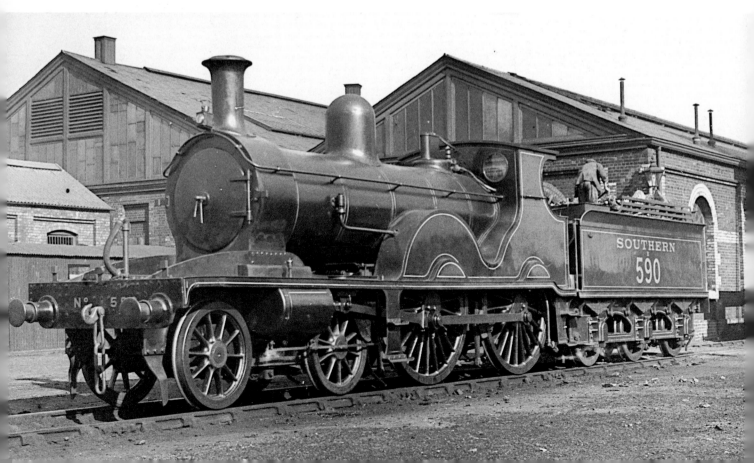

'Claughton' No. 6009 and 'Precursor' No. 5295 *Scorpion* pass Hatch End with the 'up' "Royal Scot". The LMS were going through a bad patch on the motive power front at this stage with a lack of large express engines which would not be filled until the 'Royal Scots' were available. Both engines have an 'S' on the cab side to indicate that they are suitable for use on the most important turns. Maurice Earley was with me on this occasion and I remember we went over from Reading by train. By way of contrast the other picture shows 'River' tank No. 801 *River Darenth* near Earley with the Birkenhead-Dover and Deal train, the "Continental", composed mainly of ex SECR stock but with two GWR coaches at the front. At this time the train was usually worked by one of this class. A goods for Feltham generally followed this train, sometimes used as a running in turn as shown on the picture on page 20, but more normally rostered for a Urie H16 4-6-2T which I thought were very impressive.

I am especially fond of this picture of 'King Arthur' No. 768 *Sir Balin* waiting to leave Waterloo with a semi-fast train for Basingstoke in 1925. The engine had not long been delivered from the North British Locomotive Company and is running in. I had seen it from a platform to the right of the picture and had rushed round to capture this photograph. *Sir Balin* spent its early years at Stewarts Lane shed working Continental boat expresses.

This picture was taken during a visit I made to Dover in 1929. 'Lord Nelson' No. 857 *Lord Howe* is leaving with an 'up' boat train for Victoria. Having found a good position by the lineside near some attractive signals and set our cameras up for the train, we saw a railway employee walking up the line towards us and so we thought we were going to be told to move. However it became apparent that when he concealed himself behind the wagons to the right of the picture he was more interested in watching the girls on the beach than in us!

One morning my friend Douglas Rumble came into my shop in Reading to say that 'Lord Nelson' No. 852 *Sir Walter Raleigh* was working an 'up' freight from Reading to Feltham, which for such a modern express engine was most unusual. I managed to get away from the shop long enough to take this pleasing picture of the engine having just shut off steam for a stop at Earley station where it would do some shunting. The tall pre-Grouping signal was a nice feature of this position, and I remember seeing it fall to the ground when it was replaced by a more modern version.

Like generations of railway photographers I always enjoyed a visit to Worting Junction and nearby Battledown Flyover which made an interesting background to the pictures. Here is 'Lord Nelson' No. 865 *Sir John Hawkins*, fitted with a Kylchap exhaust and double chimney, working the 'down' "Bournemouth Belle" one Sunday morning in 1938. This train was often held up behind a preceding West of England train, and so there was a chance that it would be accelerating away from a signal check to the benefit of photographers like myself. On this occasion I had cycled over from Earley with my camera on my back, but on later visits before I had a car, used the train to Basingstoke and thence a bus to Worting.

The next four pages show three of the railway photographers I met through living in Reading. In this picture Cecil Blay FRPS has his camera set up on a tripod to photograph 'Castle' No. 5094 *Tretower Castle* leaving Reading station for Paddington. Most of the photographers I knew in those days used tripods since our cameras were cumbersome and heavy, and although this practice did restrict the scope of our pictures it ensured that they were as sharp as possible, particularly since the shutter releases tended to shake the camera if you were not careful. Cecil Blay was a talented portraitist and a leading member of the Reading Camera Club.

Here is my friend Ernest Rixon photographing No. 6000 *King George V* in the 1950s on a Paddington to Birmingham train between Saunderton and Princes Risborough where the 'down' and 'up' lines run on different levels, which gives the interesting illusion of main line trains running on a branch or secondary line! Ernest has just squeezed the bulb release to the shutter of his camera and you can also see the black cloth we used to aid focussing, and to protect the glass film plates from possible fogging in bright sunlight.

Ernest again, this time on Whiteball Bank giving the thumbs up sign to the driver of 'Modified Hall' No. 6986 *Rydal Hall*, perhaps for the nice smoke effect, not very common on the Western due to the use of Welsh coal. The locomotive is working a summer Saturday train from the Midlands to South Devon. Tragically Ernest was killed in a road accident not long afterwards.

Maurice Earley was surely the most famous photographer of Great Western steam trains, and in this picture we see him at West Junction Reading with a train from the Bristol line as the subject for his camera. It is crossing over from the 'up' relief to main line with 'Modified Hall' No. 7918 *Rhose Wood Hall* piloting a 'Castle'. Maurice was always very smartly turned out, and the black coat you can see him wearing was typical – no jeans and anoraks in those days!

This was one of my favourite pictures at the time, and still is. All steam, smoke and fury on the last part of Dainton Bank. 'Hall' No. 4983 *Albert Hall* now preserved at the Birmingham Railway Museum at Tyseley, pilots a 'Castle' past Stoneycombe Quarry with a 'down' train. I was particularly pleased to capture the happy position of the ganger and his foreman to look at me at the crucial moment, and my wish was granted that they did not turn round to look at me at the crucial moment.

Dainton would invariably produce some good pictures and I made a number of visits to it, particularly on summer Saturdays when the traffic was heavy. The light was best for 'down' trains though it could be a little gloomy where the line ran through the trees as in this picture of 'Manor No. 7814 *Fringford Manor* and a 'Castle' about a quarter of a mile from Dainton Tunnel on the 1 in 44 gradient.

It was unusual to see a tank engine piloting on the Devon banks, but here is Newton Abbot's 2-6-2T No. 4145 enjoying a moment of glory on the main line in 1957. It is piloting a 'Grange' 4-6-0 on a North to West train climbing Dainton Bank at the same position as the train on the previous page, though on the other side of the line as the sun had moved round.

Another picture of 'Manor' No. 7809 *Childrey Manor* this time piloting a 'King' on the 'down' "Cornish Riviera Limited" photographed at about two o'clock, between the outer and inner distant signals, some 50 yards from the eastern portal of Dainton Tunnel.

'Castle' No. 5036 *Lyonshall Castle* makes a fine smoke effect passing Reading West Junction with the "Continental" Dover and Deal to Birkenhead train. This was my best picture at this position, and the smoke was far removed from the normal clean exhaust.

As the day progressed at Dainton the sun became ever more head-on for trains coming east as you can see from the shadow of the 'Stop Dead' board in the foreground of this picture. Nevertheless the contrajour light gives a feeling of depth to this picture of 'Castle' No. 4088 *Dartmouth Castle* nearing the tunnel with the 'up' "Royal Duchy" which left Plymouth around 2.30 pm.

From a lower viewpoint, 'Castle' No. 7029 *Clun Castle*, still with a single chimney, comes up the hill past Dainton Summit signal box with an eastbound train. You can just see a reflection of Dainton Tunnel mouth in the mirror on the signal which enabled the signalman to check that all was well with the tail lamp of an 'up' train when his view was obscured by a train on the other line.

Another picture of No. 7029 *Clun Castle*, still in original condition on the approach to Stoneycombe Quarry sidings on Dainton Bank with a neat train composed of BR Mk 1 stock.

'King' No. 6004 *King George III* although in ill-suited blue livery, makes an impressive sight in full command of a 'down' train approaching the entrance to Dainton Tunnel. Two Hawksworth coaches are behind the engine followed by **BR** Mk 1s. Although working hard, there was usually little smoke effect with these big engines, only a blue haze from the chimney.

'King' No. 6002 *King William IV* is on the other side of the Bank and about to enter Dainton Tunnel. The change to flat bottomed track on the 'down' line is marked.

A picture of a typical 'down' train of the 1950s approaching Reading to call at the General station behind 'Castle' No. 4085 *Berkeley Castle*. Assuming the train has run non-stop from Paddington it will have taken some 40 minutes to reach Reading compared with a journey time of about 25 minutes for an HST today. I was standing below East Main box and this picture gives a good view of the line down to the Southern.

Here is 'Castle' No. 7031 *Cromwell's Castle* accelerating past Southcote Junction for its run down the Berks & Hants line. The centre signal controls the Basingstoke line, and that to its left the goods branch to Coaley yard. I didn't photograph here that often as I found the signals rather ungainly.

I took this picture the wrong side for the sun to show something of the amazing array of signals at Norton Fitzwarren – 'Castle' No. 4016 *The Somerset Light Infantry (Prince Albert's)* is passing the station not long after the Second World War with a 'down' train.

'Modified Hall' No. 7924 *Thornycroft Hall* is accelerating away from Reading on an 'up' train. It was not always that easy to get the signals clear of smoke, but I have been successful here, possibly because the wind was from an easterly direction, and the engine is working vigorously in typical 'Hall' fashion.

This is one of my most successful pictures on Dainton, taken one summer Saturday in 1957 from the mound by the buffers at the end of the siding from Stoneycombe Quarry, and shows GW steam on the South Devon banks at its best. 'Manor' No. 7809 *Childrey Manor* and a 'Castle' are storming up the bank in fine style with safety valves blowing and injectors on. Note milepost 216 on the left of the picture, the distance from Paddington via Bristol.

Although the GWR was my first love, I made a number of visits to the Southern to see the Bulleid Pacifics which could not have been more different from the traditional products of Swindon. This picture was taken some 1½ miles west of Hook and shows a 'down' West of England train passing under a gantry of LSWR pneumatic signals. The engine, No. 35009 *Shaw Savill*, which is in blue livery, is in almost original condition with a curved front to the casing on to the buffer beam. Notice how perfectly the rake of Bulleid coaches match the curved profile of the tender.

Signal gantry Great Western style, with the signals 'off' at a very similar angle to the LSWR pneumatic ones. North British built 'Warship' No. D842 *Royal Oak* is leaving Reading with the 'down' "Torbay Express", whilst a 'Modified Hall' approaches from the Bristol line. At this time the train left Paddington at 12.30 pm and called at Reading 40 minutes later.

The same signal gantry as on the last page, from the other side a few years earlier but with square wooden posts and signals. 'Britannia' No. 70026 *Polar Star* is passing with the 'down' "Red Dragon" to Cardiff at about 6.30 pm when the sun was quite head-on, which could give interesting lighting effects. I used to find space for my tripod legs between the point rodding which could move at unexpected moments!

Norton Fitzwarren again, this time showing a little more of the station and the telegraph poles and wires that were once so much an accepted part of the railway scene. 'Castle' No. 5053 *Earl Cairns* on a train from the Bristol line is passing four gangers at work on the track, and the 'T' sign for the end of the permanent way restriction is visible at the end of the 'up' platform.

Looking west at Norton Fitzwarren showing the other end of the station as 'Castle' No. 5024 *Carew Castle* comes through on an 'up' train.

Cardiff (Canton) 'Britannia' No. 70029 *Shooting Star* is living up to its name as it speeds through Reading with the 'up' "Capitals United Express" which is made up of a mixture of BR and GWR stock – note that the engine has lost its right hand cylinder cover. I needed to use a high shutter speed (about 1/750th of a second) on my Mentor Reflex camera to freeze the train since it would have been travelling around 70-80 mph. The film used was HP3.

Above: 'Britannia' No. 70026 *Polar Star* is east of Reading near Kennet Bridge signal box with the 'up' train. This was the engine involved in the Milton accident which resulted in the removal of the handles on the smoke deflectors to try to improve visibility from the footplate. The locomotive is carrying the rather more ornate version of the headboard showing the crests of the City of London and Cardiff. Now of course it is difficult to tell one train from another unless you can see the small labels on the doors.

Left, top: Here is the 'down' "Capitals United" passing Tilehurst behind 'Britannia' No. 70024 *Vulcan*, hauling a set of chocolate and cream painted BR Mk 1 coaches. The line ran in a north westerly direction here, so in the late afternoon the sun was more on the side of the train than at Reading. I didn't like that pole but it was difficult to avoid from this position.

Left: Before the 'Castles' were ousted from Canton by the 'Britannias', No. 4073 *Caerphilly Castle* passes Reading with the 'up' train – note the blow from the right hand of the middle cylinders. Whilst I was sorry to see the 'Castles' lose this turn to the 'Britannias', I liked the look of the new engines with their interesting Walschaerts valve gear and exposed wheels which could be more photogenic than the plain looking GWR arrangement.

The 'up' train just west of Pangbourne behind 'Britannia' No. 70025 *Western Star*. This locomotive was one of five allocated to Cardiff (Canton) shed in 1952 where the conservative Western men made the best use of them, despite the unfamiliarity of the left hand driving position. Although the semaphore signals have gone, this is still a nice location and the trees are particularly beautiful in the autumn.

The "Bristol Pullman" ran on Mondays to Fridays between Paddington and Bristol (Temple Meads), and the shape of the train anticipated the design of the HSTs by some years. This picture is of the 12.45 pm train from Paddington passing Reading on its two hour run to Bristol.

Left top: 'Castle' No. 7035 *Ogmore Castle* has just left Alderton Tunnel with the 'down' "South Wales Pullman". The first time I went to this location to photograph this train was by means of a taxi from Chippenham which dropped my by a bridge from where I walked along the line towards the tunnel. I set up my camera for the "Pullman" but the picture was ruined by two scruffy, ordinary maroon painted coaches next to the engine! However on this occasion everything was all right.

Above: The steam hauled equivalent of the "Bristol Pullman", was the "Bristolian" which left Paddington at 8.45 am for a two hour run to Bristol, stopping only at Bath, whereas some "Bristol Pullman" trains stopped at Chippenham as well. The "Bristolian" was a light train to allow the 'Castle' to meet the fast two hour schedule, and it was not unknown for the train to top 100 mph on the descent of Dauntsey Bank on the 'down' run to the delight of those on board timing the train. In this picture a 'Castle' makes a pleasing picture sprinting along near 'Two Turn Bridge', Pangbourne one misty morning with the 'down' train.

Left: More traditional in appearance was the "South Wales Pullman", here photographed passing Patchway, very slowly I remember, behind 'Castle' No. 5077 *Fairey Battle* embellished with white buffers and coupling hook.

Some old GWR wooden signals are surviving in this picture of 'Star' No. 4036 *Queen Elizabeth* snaking out of Reading past East Main box with a train for Paddington. Note the small 'calling-on' signal on the signal post. You can also see the big window at the end of the box which was a favourite vantage point of mine for taking 'down' trains arriving in the station.

Opposite: 'Castle' No. 5084 *Reading Abbey* makes a powerful start from Reading with a train for the Bristol line – the signalman has been very quick off the mark to put his signals back up on the gantry in the background. It was possible to set up the camera quite safely once the road had been set for the Bristol line, and I always liked the look of the trackwork at this busy junction.

I liked to get the attractive GWR signals in my pictures if I could, and this picture of 'Castle' No. 5090 *Neath Abbey* preparing for a stop at Exeter St. David's with a 'down' train is a typical example.

This picture gives a good idea of the attractive countryside on the Somerset/Devon border which sets off a 'Warship' diesel hydraulic climbing to Whiteball with the 'down' ''Cornish Riviera Express'' just short of the tunnel. The train is made up of BR Mk 1 coaches but with two GWR restaurant car vehicles. In the background you can just make out Sampford Arundel church. Ernest Rixon has decided on a close in shot and the locomotive has just passed him. Some other pictures in this book are taken from the opposite side of the line and show the colour light signal on the 'up' side. We knew that a diesel would be working the train and my idea was to get the whole thing in from high up on the embankment.

'King' class No. 6008 *King James II* passes the Whiteball 'down' distant signal close to the tunnel mouth with the "Cornish Riviera Limited" – note the different nameboard to the train opposite. This picture was published in the *Western Region Magazine*.

'King' No. 6004 *King George III* is on the 'down' relief line in Sonning Cutting one Sunday morning with the 'down' "Cornish Riviera Limited". The train is composed of BR Mk 1 stock except for the two GWR restaurant cars. Because of engineering works nothing came along on the two main lines and I could almost have set up my camera between them.

This picture too was published in the *Western Region Magazine* and *Holiday Haunts*, and shows 'Two Ways to Plymouth', with the 'down' "Cornish Riviera" at Cowley Bridge Junction, Exeter passing a Southern train which is using the route via Okehampton. On first glance you might think I was exceptionally lucky to get these two trains in exactly the right position, but in fact I cheated by taking two separate pictures without moving the camera, printed them, and then prepared a montage of the two which I re-photographed to produce one negative. I think the result is fairly convincing. On the day I was due to take the photograph I reported to a Mr. Robinson I think it was, at Exeter St. David's who arranged for me to be escorted up the line to Cowley Bridge Junction. He was very helpful but I couldn't help laughing when he said, "But I warn you, I'm not stopping any trains"!

A look at a Western Region timetable for the 1950s and early 1960s will detail over 15 named trains, and the next ten pages show a selection of these, starting with the "Royal Duchy", Paddington to Penzance, pictured here arriving at Reading behind 'Castle' No. 5092 *Tresco Abbey*. Photographically the named trains were more interesting and I tried to photograph as many as I could.

Further down the line 'Castle' No. 4037 *The South Wales Borderers* with its distinctive nameplate and crest, is leaving Whiteball Tunnel with the 'down' "Torbay Express" bound for Kingswear. At this period the tasteful train nameboards on Brunswick green engines with their copper fitments, and the neat sets of **BR Mk 1** stock painted in the old GWR colours, made a lovely sight.

'King' No. 6000 *King George V* is accelerating through Reading with the 'up' "Mayflower" from Plymouth, which arrived at Paddington around 1.20 pm. To the left of the picture is Southern Region Class 4 4-6-0 No. 76062 which for some reason has a board showing 'Victoria' above its buffer beam!

I never found the 'Counties' quite as photogenic as the 'Castles' or 'Kings', and it looked to me as though someone had sat on them, but they were quite business-like locomotives. No. 1009 *County of Carmarthen* is in charge of the 'down' 'Cornishman', one of the principal Midlands to South Devon trains which ran from Wolverhampton to Penzance. The train is climbing the 1 in 80 gradient on the approach to Whiteball Tunnel. The pointed conifer in the background is still there to my knowledge, and you had to be careful where it appeared in the photograph.

A picture which recalls lovely summer days on the South Wales line when the distinctive shape of the English elm added so much to the landscape. 'Britannia' No. 70027 *Rising Star* is in charge of the 'up' "Red Dragon", Carmarthen to Paddington about one mile east of Badminton. Sadly those elms were the victim of Dutch elm disease and have now been cut down.

As its name suggested the "Merchant Venturer" ran from Paddington to Bath and Bristol, and here the train makes a fine picture crossing the junction with the Berks & Hants line at Reading. To the left a 'Hall' 4-6-0 approaches the station, whilst in the far distance a Drummond 4-4-0, possibly a D15, is waiting to leave for the Basingstoke line. I am standing on a concrete buffer stop which provided an excellent vantage point for photography.

On a lovely clear morning in spring, a beautifully turned out 'Castle' makes a fine picture speeding through Reading with the 'up' "Cheltenham Spa Express". On days like these I would try to get away from the shop for a short time to take a picture or two while the light was at its best.

The "Pembroke Coast Express" was the South Wales equivalent of the "Cambrian Coast Express" which ran north-west out of Paddington. As its name implied, the "Pembroke Coast Express" started at Pembroke Dock and took nearly seven hours to reach Paddington where it was due around 7.45 pm. The train is approaching Patchway behind a 'Castle' after the steep climb from Severn Tunnel.

Over on the line to Birmingham and Wolverhampton during a visit made with Maurice Earley and Ernest Rixon, a 'King' speeds north-west between Saunderton and Princes Risborough with the 'down' "Inter City", 8.20 am from Paddington.

On the same occasion here is the "Cambrian Coast Express" on the first stage of its long journey to Aberystwyth and Pwllheli, at the same position hauled by a very smartly turned out Old Oak Common 'Castle', No. 5056 *Earl of Powis*. The scene is little changed here today, though the permanent way hut has gone, and there is more lineside vegetation. After stopping at most stations up the Cambrian coast from Machynlleth, the Pwllheli portion eventually ran into the north-west Wales resort at nearly eight o'clock in the evening, too late for dinner!

Cecil Blay and I often used to go together to Sonning Cutting where the birch trees made an attractive frame for the trains. Here a 'Castle' is speeding through with a Worcester line train. The two bridges in the background carry Main Road, Sonning and Warren Lane.

A lovely springtime picture of 'King' No. 6016 *King Edward V* entering Sonning Cutting with the 'up' "Mayflower" composed of Mk 1 British Railways standard coaches in chocolate and cream.

One of my favourite pictures of an 'up' stopping train breasting the summit of Dainton Bank from the west – the 1 in 37 gradient can clearly be seen in the background. 'Castle' No. 5059 *Earl of St. Aldwyn* from Newton Abbot shed is making a last effort, with whistle blowing for the passage through the tunnel. The locomotive seems to be leaking badly from the middle cylinders which may explain why it is not on a main line duty.

On a hot summer day 'Castle' No. 4086 *Builth Castle* is coming through Sonning Cutting with a short seven coach 'up' train including some 'Centenary' stock with recessed doors.

Once again the trees give depth to this picture of a rare visitor to Sonning, 'Rebuilt Royal Scot' No. 46168 *The Girl Guide* which is working a Guide special from Windsor Central to the North. I had heard that this train was due but could not get away from business in time to position myself in the best location.

Widening the angle near the same place as No. 46168 gives a totally different perspective, and the locomotive is set off well by the neatly cut embankment on the 'up' side of the line. 'Britannia' No. 70024 *Vulcan* is on a South Wales train.

There is no mistaking the great sweep of the nameplate of this 'Castle', No. 5069 *Isambard Kingdom Brunel*, coming through Sonning Cutting with the 'down' "Royal Duchy" and making more smoke than was usual with South Wales coal. This is one of my favourite pictures in Sonning.

It is a sunny Sunday morning and 'Castle' No. 5019 *Treago Castle* from Bristol (Bath Road) shed is running in after overhaul at Swindon works. The train is using the 'up' relief line, and is about to go under the Main Road bridge in Sonning Cutting.

Also on the 'up' relief line is 'Castle' No. 5075 *Wellington* with a train from Gloucester which has just passed the picturesque Warren Lane Bridge, which has featured in so many classic pictures at Sonning. In the background is Sonning Main Road bridge where the picture of No. 5019 was taken.

In lovely clear light 'Modified Hall' No. 7921 *Edstone Hall* passes a signal gantry near Reading with a 'down' coal train.

'Hall' No. 4913 *Baglan Hall* is passing a nice signal gantry soon after leaving Reading with an 'up' vans train. The headlamp on the engine appears to be incorrect showing 'Class G' light engine, whereas it should be 'Class C'. Reading General station can be seen in the background.

I was rather pleased with this picture of Didcot shed's Churchward 4300 class 2-6-0 No. 7327 which I took west of Pangbourne on the 'up' main line with a long express freight. The soft winter light has given an especially attractive effect.

2800 class 2-8-0 No. 2800 itself is forging steadily ahead up Dainton Bank with a semi-fitted freight train, with about seven cattle wagons behind the engine. In later years when 'Liner' trains and bulk loads were normal, I missed the photogenic long slow freights composed of four wheeled wagons.

Following the passage of an 'up' express, 2-8-0 No. 2822 climbs slowly through Patchway with an unfitted freight train banked in the rear from its passage through the Severn Tunnel by a tank locomotive.

Occupied in chatting to a ganger at Scours Lane near Reading, I almost missed this rare sight of 'Castle' No. 4083 *Abbotsbury Castle* working an 'up' freight train.

Because of a landslip on the Southern Region main line at Hook, a number of interesting trains were diverted via Basingstoke and Reading, which enabled me to take this picture of Urie S15 No. 30502 about to pull away from Spur Junction for Feltham. I did not take as many pictures on the Southern Region's line from Reading South since being a secondary route, it lacked main line engines and the variety you could see on the Western side.

Sister engine No. 30509 makes an attractive picture coasting under the gantry of signals at the west end of Basingstoke station with a freight for Southampton Docks. I spent quite a bit of time at Basingstoke, sometimes en route to Worting Junction and Battledown.

A striking picture of 'Hall' No. 6944 *Fledborough Hall* emerging from Dainton Tunnel with a westbound freight train. I had set up my camera near the tunnel mouth for a picture of a train coming out, and fortunately this 'Hall' emerged at a walking pace ready to stop to pin down brakes for the descent towards Totnes.

94

I always thought that the Urie H16 4-6-2Ts were most impressive locomotives with a look of indestructibility. Just before taking this picture I was walking along the Western Region main line when I saw this freight for Feltham hauled by No. 30520 about to leave the Southern Spur yard by the gasworks at Reading. Nipping across I had time to ask the fireman to try to make some smoke as the train pulled out, and this is the result.

The Southern Region's Reading South station was very much eclipsed by the Western establishment across the road with its constant procession of gleaming 'Kings' and 'Castles'. Rather more mundane is Maunsell 'U' class No. 31612 leaving the South station at the start of the attractive cross country trip to Guildford and Redhill, 46 miles on. The rolling stock of one SECR 'Birdcage' set is typical for this line in the 1950s and early 1960s.

Nearly 40 years have passed since I took this picture of 'King Arthur' No. 30777 *Sir Lamiel* plodding past Battledown Flyover with a heavy freight for Southampton Docks. Although the locomotive shows the first signs of Nationalisation with 'BRITISH RAILWAYS' painted on the tender and a smokebox numberplate, it lacks a shedplate, retaining instead the legend 'E'LGH' on the buffer beam.

Like No. 30777, rebuilt 'Merchant Navy' No. 35005 *Canadian Pacific* survives, and is currently undergoing restoration at Carnforth. Here is the locomotive leaving Winchfield one Sunday morning with a Salisbury to Waterloo train.

Anticipating the regalia it would sometimes carry in later preservation, 'West Country' Pacific No. 34092 *City of Wells* stands under the coaling stage at Stewarts Lane shed before backing down to Victoria to work the "Golden Arrow". I always liked this picture and did a 20 in x 16 in exhibition print which gave me, and others I hope, a great deal of pleasure.

The arches at Stewarts Lane provided a very strong setting for photographing the locomotives waiting to take coal and water. One of the depot's 'Schools' No. 30908 *Westminster* poses for my camera below the blackened bricks of the viaduct.

Left, top: I did not visit the London Midland Region very much due to lack of spare time more than anything else, but here is a picture I took at Nuneaton shed during a visit with Maurice Earley's Railway Photographic Society. This shows Fairburn 2-6-4T No. 42106 standing outside the shed waiting for its next turn of duty.

Above: Another favourite spot of mine was Liverpool Street station and its locomotive depot. The gentleman operating the turntable was always very obliging and would hold the locomotive on the turntable almost as long as I wished, such as in this picture of B17/6 No. 61659 *East Anglian* from Yarmouth shed. This was one of the B17s that had been streamlined by Gresley in 1937.

Left: After the war I became especially interested in pictorial studies of shed details, and I liked looking for pictures such as this one of a water crane at Stratford shed on the Eastern Region. I used my Rolleiflex camera and found its large clear screen ideal for composing pictures such as this.

Above: All the dirt and atmosphere of the steam shed comes across I think in this picture of 2-6-4T No. 42088 and H class No. 31551 under the coaling tower at Stewarts Lane shed. The tank of No. 42088 has been filled and the driver is about to pull the water hose away.
104

Right: One of my best known pictures, a powerful study taken with my Rolleiflex of 'Battle of Britain' Pacific No. 34071 *601 Squadron* under the coaling tower at Stewarts Lane. I used the camera on a tripod, and the slow shutter speed has enhanced the rolling effect of the smoke pouring out of the chimney to mingle with the girders of the coaling tower. This picture was exhibited at a Royal Photographic Society exhibition where it was described as one of the outstanding pictures, illustrating the formidable strength of the locomotive.
105

At Camden shed a driver comes off shift and walks past work stained 'Princess Royal' Pacific No. 46204 *Princess Louise* from Edge Hill shed. This picture was taken during a Railway Photographic Society visit.

I always liked to take pictures of staff preparing locomotives for service as in this picture of 'Battle of Britain' Pacific No. 34087 *145 Squadron* at Stewarts Lane in the early 1950s.

A very different outline was to be seen at King's Cross shed in the shape of A4 Pacific No. 60006 *Sir Ralph Wedgwood*, also being prepared for a train. Note the clean condition of the area between the rails.

Stewarts Lane Pacific No. 70004 *William Shakespeare* was kept in especially fine condition for working the "Golden Arrow", and is being given the full cleaning treatment before running light to Victoria to pick up the train. One cleaner is burnishing the copper pipes on the injector, and the foreman is fixing the Union and Tricolour flags on the front of the locomotive. Looking at the smoky surroundings of the shed the engine must have needed a thorough clean every day.

I have already mentioned No. 70004 and the "Golden Arrow" in the picture on the previous page. Here is the beautiful result – Richard Hardy, the then shedmaster at Stewarts Lane agreed that the engine might be posed under the coaling stage, but only for a minute or so in case it became dirty before going down to Victoria for the train.

WILLIAM SHAKESPEARE

In the days of steam over the South Devon banks, Newton Abbot shed was a very busy one. Here some of the shed staff are cleaning the depot's 'Castle' No. 4099 *Kilgerran Castle* in the traditional way with cotton waste soaked in paraffin. The GWR pattern 'Not to be Moved' boards are especially attractive.

Strong head-on light at Ranelagh Bridge depot, and smoke rolling from the chimney make for a powerful picture of 'Castle' No. 7034 *Ince Castle* waiting for its next turn of duty. I spent many happy hours in this location, a fine spot for photographs with big engines coming and going all the time. On a summer day as the sun moved round, there were many opportunities for pleasing photographs.

Front ends at Ranelagh Bridge depot – 'Halls' No. 6796 *Graythwaite Hall* and No. 5993 *Kirby Hall*, and 'King' No. 6016 *King Edward V*. All my pictures at this location were taken with my Rolleiflex camera which was quick, accurate and effective to use for this sort of work.

An attractive line-up of front ends at King's Cross shed one Sunday with A4 Pacific No. 60006 *Sir Ralph Wedgwood* and No. 60032 *Gannet*, together with Immingham 'Britannia' No. 70035 *Rudyard Kipling* which will have worked in with a train from Grimsby.

Left: County 4-6-0s in their original condition – an early unidentified member of the class still un-named, is at Penzance shed (top), and No. 1026 *County of Salop* is at Wolverhampton (below).

Above: One of the greatly admired Churchward 2-8-0s No. 4701 from Old Oak Common shed is waiting its next turn of duty in Tyseley roundhouse, where it was unusual to see one.

Left: At Eastleigh Works Bulleid 'West Country' Pacific No. 34034 *Honiton* makes an interesting picture as it undergoes attention. Note the mechanical lubricators above the buffer beam, the young lad to the left of the engine, possibly an apprentice, and the unusually perfect condition of the casing on the side of the locomotive which was invariably less than flat. Right at the back of the shop is what appears to be the cab of an Adams locomotive, and to the side of 34034 is 'King Arthur' No. 30781 *Sir Aglovale*.

Above: Also at Eastleigh three fitters are at work in the smokebox of Adams 02 class 0-4-4T No. 30223 built in 1892, which forms a contrast to No. 34034. Note the comparatively crude but effective way in which the engine is jacked up on the wood blocks, and the 700 class chimney on the left hand side of the picture. The lighting was so good from the glass roof of the works that I did not need a tripod.

Above: These ex Ministry of Supply, Austerity 2-8-0s added to the interest at Great Western depots after the war, and I was pleased to get this picture of one of the class having its smokebox cleaned out between duties at Reading shed, about 1947.

Right: I was walking round Stewarts Lane shed during a visit, when I suddenly came on this scene of a Fairburn 2-6-4T, No. 42088 having its tubes cleaned and which I captured with my Rolleiflex using HP3 film. The picture was unposed and I sent a copy to the fitter who was delighted with the result, as I was.

Above: Back over at Ranelagh Bridge depot by Paddington, Cardiff (Canton) 'Britannia' No. 70028 *Royal Star* is not in quite such immaculate condition as Stewarts Lane's No. 70004, but nevertheless in very smart order for working the 'down' "Red Dragon". After asking a driver for permission to photograph him, I would take one shot, and then when he had relaxed and become quite natural, take the real one!

Right, top: A friendly GWR footplate crew at Plymouth Laira about 1946. This is driver Gordard and his fireman standing in front of their 'Castle' No. 5050 *Earl of St. Germans* on which they had given me a lift from the North Road station to the shed.

Right: At Reading shed I was lucky to be able to photograph 'Britannia' No. 70020 *Mercury* in brand new condition from Crewe, on a local running in turn. The enginemen seem proud of their new charge judging by their postures and the look on their faces. The locomotive has not yet received a shedplate. I secured this picture through the good offices of Mr. Lloyd the then shedmaster at Reading who I got to know well. He was a tough old boy, but very helpful and would ring me up at my shop and say in his booming voice, "John, I've got so-and-so on the shed at the moment" – if I could get away from the shop for a bit I would be on my bike and off. Service with a smile I called it!

Above: The lighting at Ranelagh Bridge depot could sometimes give some lovely effects, as on 'Castle' No. 5015 *Kingswear Castle* waiting to work a train up to Birmingham and Wolverhampton where it was shedded. Whilst talking to a driver I turned round and saw that the sun had lit the engine and wagon just as I wanted.
125

Right: I know the top picture may be familiar to some, but it is one of my favourites which I had to include. Bill Lennie, the foreman at Ranelagh Bridge depot appears to be pushing single handed, 'King' No. 6008 *King James II* of Wolverhampton shed. He was very co-operative and this occasion I had asked him to adopt a position of strength which he has done well. In the other picture, 'Britannia' No. 70027 *Rising Star* from Cardiff (Canton) is ready to work back to South Wales. The houses behind the engine provided an interesting but fairly unobtrusive and neutral background.
126/127

Times had changed at Swindon works when I took this picture in the early 1960s. No longer were there lines of 'Kings' and 'Castles', but three diesel hydraulics, from the left a North British 'Warship' No. D603 *Conquest,* Class 22 No. D6329, and a D800 series 'Warship'. Conditions look almost hygienic compared to the days when the works dealt exclusively with steam, and I missed the photogenic wheels, connecting rods and so forth from 'Castles', 'Kings' and other main line steam classes. I also

had an interesting day or two at Swindon works helping Walter Nurnberg FRPS with his lighting for an assignment he was undertaking. Walter came to this country in the 1930s from Germany, and after the war, made a name for himself as an Industrial Photographer with a special interest in lighting effects.

Brown Boveri Gas Turbine No. 18000 was almost new when I took this picture of it leaving Reading for Bristol, and I think this was the first time I had seen it. The man on the left hand side of the cab is probably a travelling engineer, and the locomotive looks so highly polished that there is a perfect reflection of the man riding in the rear cab. The steam type whistle looks incongruous on the cab roof. I have read recently that this locomotive still survives in Vienna, and pictures of it show the 'steam' whistle still in place.

One of the original series of five North British built diesel hydraulics, No. D603 *Conquest*, revs its engines as it starts from Penzance with the 'up' "Cornish Riviera Express". These locomotives were not as successful as the later D800 series 'Warships' and D1000 series 'Westerns', but their arrival in 1958 marked the beginning of the end of steam on main line traction on the Western Region. The last years of their service on the Western Region were mainly spent working west of Plymouth on duties such as the one in this picture.

Transition from steam to diesel on the Western Region – one cold winter morning a D1000 series 'Western' diesel hydraulic is passing Reading West Junction with an 'up' train from the Bristol line, whilst a Churchward 2-6-0 stands in the yard to the north. I was up a signal post and was waiting to photograph a block load freight train.

A little while later two Birmingham RC&W Co. Type 3 (Class 33) diesel electric with No. D6525 leading, take the line to Reading West with an Esso petrol tanker train, probably bound for Fawley. Reading West Junction box can be seen in the background.

This picture was taken from Reading West Junction signal box and shows a new Brush Type 4 (Class 47) diesel electric No. D1682 on what seems to be a crew training working.

Even in their declining years, the D1000 class were not often seen on loose coupled freight trains, but here is No. D1052 *Western Viceroy* coming under the signal gantry at West Main Junction Reading with such a train.

Left: Two pictures of an early 'Warship', No. D601 *Ark Royal,* the first arriving at Reading with the 'up' "Cornish Riviera Express", and the second leaving Reading for Paddington. I would have much preferred to have seen a 'King' or 'Castle' on the train, but we had to make the best of the new motive power, and in any case with the passage of time these photos of early Western Region diesel power have a fascination in their own right.

Above: In the opposite direction, 'Warship' diesel hydraulic No. D806 *Cambrian* is approaching Reading with the 'down' "Royal Duchy". To the right of the picture Churchward 2-6-0 No. 7331 is waiting for access to the main line.

The Type 3 'Hymeks', (Class 35), were built by Beyer Peacock from 1961 to 1964 and took over many workings previously handled by 'Hall' or 'Castle' 4-6-0s, notably on the Paddington – Worcester trains. Here No. D7026, which went into traffic in 1962, is arriving at Reading with an 'up' train passing West Main box.

Although not so impressive as a 'King', the D1000 'Western' class were nevertheless striking locomotives, especially to the eyes of observers in 1961 used to less angular lines. This is the first member of the class No. D1000 *Western Enterprise* in almost new condition arriving at High Wycombe with an 'up' train. Strangely enough I do not actually remember taking this picture, but I think I had gone to High Wycombe to get some shots of trains with the attractive wall in the background and this locomotive came along.

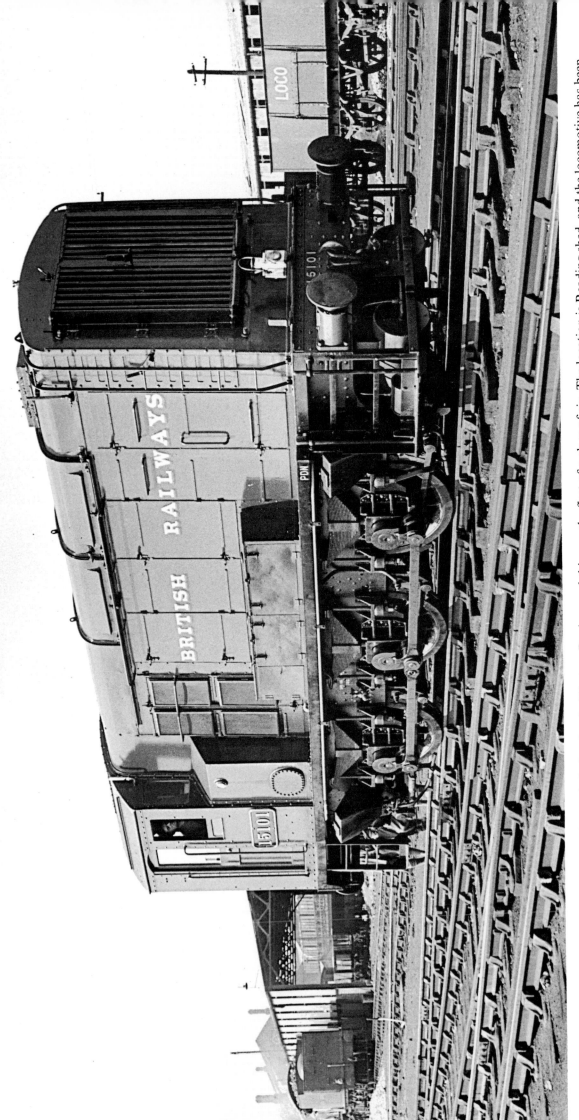

No. 15101 was an English Electric and Hawksworth design for the Western Region, and this was the first of a class of six. The location is Reading shed, and the locomotive has been 'Westernised' to the extent that it is in green livery, has a cast numberplate on the cab side and a buffer beam number. Note the code 'PDN' on the side of the frames, and the locomotive probably ex works from Swindon and en route to Old Oak Common. I was coming back in the train and saw this diesel in the yard as I passed, so I walked back along the line to photograph it.

Climbing steadily up the 1 in 100 from the Severn Tunnel, 2-8-0 No. 3840 passes Cattybrook sidings with a heavy coal train from South Wales, banked in the rear by a tank engine, and will soon enter the 'up' single track bore of Patchway Tunnel.

In the late afternoon sunshine, an immaculate Landore 'Castle' No. 5077 *Fairey Battle* is passing Cattybrook sidings with the 'up' "Pembroke Coast Express". This train was running late and I had waited in the signal box for it. At least I knew when it was coming, since I had ordered a taxi to take me back from Cattybrook to Bristol to catch my train home!

'Britannia' No. 70018 *Flying Dutchman* is photographed near Patchway with an 'up' express from South Wales. The tunnel mouth can be seen in the background.

Above: One of my favourite pictures, which shows a small Emett like tank engine *Penlee* (Freudenstein 73 of 1901, 0-4-0 well tank) engaged in some shunting of china clay wagons at Newlyn in 1939. We were on holiday in Cornwall, and whilst walking along the quay came upon this scene which was made especially attractive with the shafts of light slanting through the dust as the clay was loaded into the hold of the boat.

Right: I was fortunate to be able to visit Earley Power Station, Reading after the last war and to get these two pictures of resident 0-4-0ST locomotive No. 1, (Stephenson & Hawthorns 7058 of 1942). I asked the driver to make some smoke for me as he pulled out of the sidings, but as sometimes happens with these arrangements, he shut off too soon!

An exciting time for me was the appearance at Reading of 'foreign' engines during the 1948 Locomotive Exchanges. Both the trains shown are the 1.30 pm Paddington to Plymouth in charge of the famous Gresley A4 Pacific No. 22 *Mallard*, and 'Rebuilt Royal Scot' No. 46162 *Queen's Westminster Rifleman*. The trains are just about to turn onto the Berks & Hants line. Of course I made a special visit to the station to take these pictures and as it turned out it was the only chance I had.

Another special occasion was when Eastern Region V2 class No. 60845 underwent some controlled tests with very heavy loads on the Western Region from Reading to Severn Tunnel Junction. Here is the train waiting to leave Reading West Junction on a westbound run, with my friend, Inspector Rixon on the far right hand side of the picture.

'Rebuilt Royal Scot' locomotive No. 46111 *Royal Fusilier* gets to grips with Camden Bank on a train for Manchester. This picture was taken during a visit by the Railway Photographic Society to Camden shed.

Above: Also coming up Camden Bank is 'Duchess' Pacific No. 46255 *City of Hereford* taken on the same occasion as the previous picture. The crew of the locomotive had agreed to make some smoke as they came towards us but unfortunately were almost checked to a stand just down the line, and were moving too slowly for anything worthwhile to come out of the chimney.

Right, top: This picture was taken during a visit to the Lickey Incline with a party from my son's school, and shows 'Jubilee' No. 45660 *Rooke* preparing to tackle the 1 in 37 bank with a train for Birmingham.

Right: Class 5 No. 44981 passes Chesterfield with a fitted freight train. I was spending a week's holiday with Cecil Blay at Matlock, where we were taking mainly pictorial studies of scenery. There was so much steam about then it did not bother me to spend time photographing away from the railway since you always knew there would be another day!

I always liked Liverpool Street station where good light and shade pictures were to be had, and as at Reading I became very friendly with the station staff. The shunter in the picture stood looking up the line for many minutes, perhaps seeking information about the next duties for N7/4 class 0-6-2T No. 69614 and J69/1 class 0-6-0T No. 68631.

Class **B1** No. 61301 from Cambridge shed makes a pleasant picture waiting for its next turn of duty at Liverpool Street. The locomotive is fitted with electric lighting supplied from the small steam operated generator on the right hand side of the smokebox.

Left, top: A typical light and shade effect in the smoky sunlight at Liverpool Street. B12 No. 61571 waits to leave with a train for the Ipswich line.

Above: The 'Britannia' Pacifics were an attractive feature of Liverpool Street and I enjoyed photographing these powerful machines in the small depot by the station, and I remember the first one that I saw was No. 70013 *Oliver Cromwell*. No. 70002 *Geoffrey Chaucer* is seen here waiting to work the return "Broadsman" train, 3.30 pm from Liverpool Street to Sheringham where it arrived just after 7 pm.

Left: The front end of B17/6 No. 61665 *Leicester City* makes for a satisfying study at Liverpool Street depot. I liked to get in close sometimes when the light was good to try to achieve the maximum impact. I had intended to take some pictures at the tunnels outside the station, but became more interested in the lighting effects and opportunities at the depot.

No. 70009 *Alfred the Great* looks especially impressive at Liverpool Street as the lighting emphasises its powerful proportions. No. 70009 was one of three 'Britannias' sent on loan to the Southern Region in 1951, and regularly worked the "Bournemouth Belle" for a while.

'Britannia' "007" at Liverpool Street, perhaps appropriately named *Coeur-de-Lion!* The locomotive is ready to leave with a train for the Norwich line. It all worked for me at Liverpool Street, the engines, the lighting, the attractive station and the friendly staff. Of course if I had been able to take more time off from business I would have visited other locations, but as it was I had to content myself with a few, but which I covered to my satisfaction.

Above: Here is a 'down' fitted freight about to enter Whiteball Tunnel in charge of 'Hall' No. 4914 *Cranmore Hall* from Bristol (St. Philip's Marsh) shed. I am standing right up against the ganger's hut at the entrance to the tunnel.

Right, top: The 'Modified Hall' class were useful motive power for a variety of turns including express working, typified by No. 7917 *North Aston Hall* on an 'up' train passing Kennet Bridge box, east of Reading.

Right: Near Pangbourne, 'Hall' No. 6945 *Glasfryn Hall* brings an 'up' parcels train along this delightful stretch of line from Didcot. The river is on the right and the bridge takes a farm track under the line. This was a good place on summer afternoons when the sun had moved round to a broadside position.

The Liverpool Street pilot again, N7/4 class 0-6-2T No. 69614, this time in the highly burnished condition which made it such a

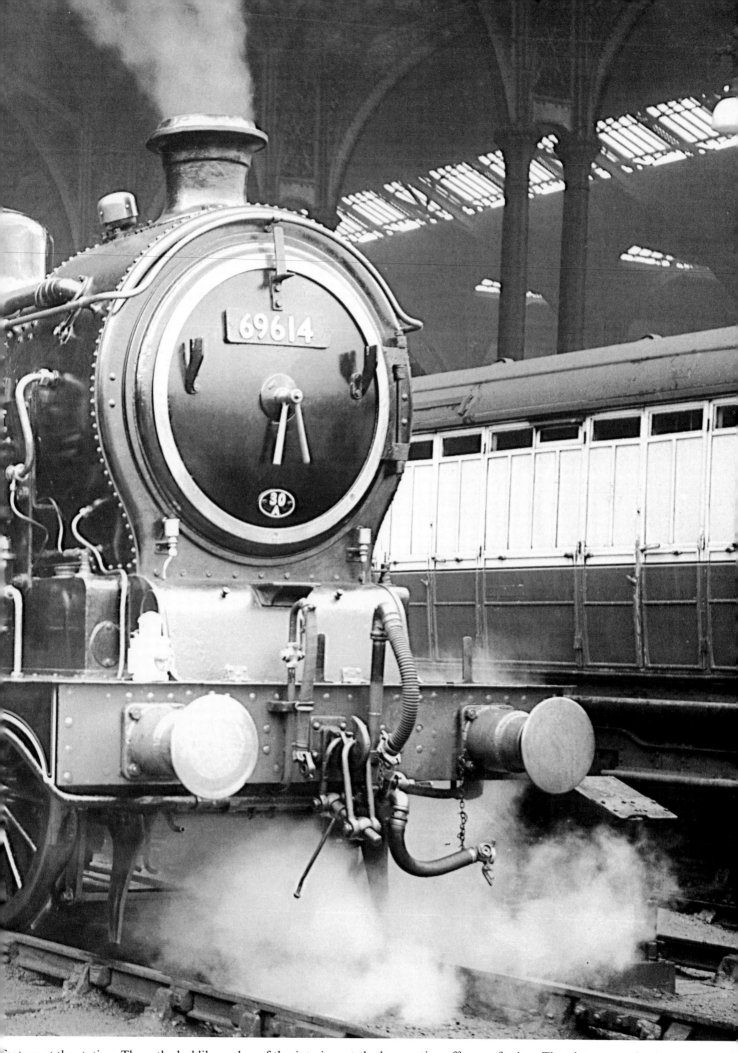

feature at the station. The cathedral like arches of the interior set the locomotive off to perfection. The picture says it all.

A 'King' passing Whiteball box to the south of the tunnel with an unusually short train for Plymouth, and is beginning the 20 miles or so descent to Exeter St. David's station.

Dramatic light sets off this picture of 'King' No. 6021 *King Richard II* coasting into Reading where it will stop with this South Wales train. Visually I much preferred the 'Kings' when fitted with a single chimney as the long proportions of the double version seemed to throw the front end out of balance.

An unusual event at Reading – 'King' No. 6009 *King Charles II* has disgraced itself by failing with a small fault on an 'up' train, and a 'Hall' was quickly substituted for the remainder of the run to Paddington. The 'King' took over the 'Hall' duty and is engaged on some light shunting in Reading lower yard. Note the express headlamps. Not only did I get this picture but also a ride on the footplate back to Reading General station when the 'King' returned to the shed for attention.

The two distant signals set off this evening picture of No. 4088 *Dartmouth Castle* heading through Sonning Cutting with the 'down' "Cathedrals Express", 5.15 pm from Paddington to Worcester and Hereford. On a summer evening the sun moved to a head-on position which could produce some nice lighting conditions, before setting on the north side of the line, though by that time the cutting would be in shadow.

The "Cheltenham Spa Express" left 15 minutes before the "Cathedrals Express" with a first stop at Kemble. Here is the train heading into the evening sun near Pangbourne behind 'Hall' No. 5907 *Marble Hall*. The sun was less head on here than at Sonning in the evening but nevertheless could be very striking.

I just happened to be down at Sonning when 'Hall' No. 6906 *Chicheley Hall* came through the cutting with a 'down' special train composed of Eastern Region stock.

The charm and easy going pace of a country branch connection is crystallised in this study of pannier tank No. 9605 taking water at Savernake with a train for Marlborough. I sometimes wonder if I missed anything by not taking branch line pictures, but compared with the action and excitement of main line steam, and the pictorial effects one could find at large sheds, their appeal to me was not so great.